J 976.4 H218
Hamilton, Joh
Texas : the Lo

P9-DNG-311

TEXAS

The Lone Star State

BY
JOHN HAMILTON

Abdo & Daughters

An imprint of Abdo Publishing | abdopublishing.com

abdopublishing.com

Published by ABDO Publishing, a division of ABDO, PO Box 398166, Minneapolis, Minnesota 55439. Copyright © 2017 by Abdo Consulting Group, Inc. International copyrights reserved in all countries. No part of this book may be reproduced in any form without written permission from the publisher. ABDO & Daughters™ is a trademark and logo of ABDO Publishing.

Printed in the United States of America, North Mankato, Minnesota.
072016
092016

THIS BOOK CONTAINS
RECYCLED MATERIALS

Editor: Sue Hamilton   **Contributing Editor:** Bridget O'Brien
Graphic Design: Sue Hamilton
Cover Art Direction: Candice Keimig   **Cover Photo Selection:** Neil Klinepier
Cover Photo: iStock
Interior Images: Alamy, AP, Dallas Cowboys, Dallas Mavericks, Dallas Stars, Dallas-Fort Worth International Airport, Dreamstime, Getty, Granger, History in Full Color-Restoration/ Colorization, Houston Astros, Houston Rockets, Houston Texans, iStock, John Hamilton, Library of Congress, Mile High Maps, Minden Pictures, Mountain High Maps, NASA, NOAA, One Mile Up, San Antonio Spurs, San Antonio Stars, Six Flags Over Texas, State Fair of Texas, Texas A&M University, Texas Historical Commission, Texas Parks & Wildlife, Texas Rangers, White House, Wikimedia

Statistics: *State and City Populations*, U.S. Census Bureau, July 1, 2015 estimates; *Land and Water Area*, U.S. Census Bureau, 2010 Census, MAF/TIGER database; *State Temperature Extremes*, NOAA National Climatic Data Center; *Climatology and Average Annual Precipitation*, NOAA National Climatic Data Center, 1980-2015 statewide averages; *State Highest and Lowest Points*, NOAA National Geodetic Survey.

Websites: To learn more about the United States, visit booklinks.abdopublishing.com. These links are routinely monitored and updated to provide the most current information available.

Cataloging-in-Publication Data

Names: Hamilton, John, 1959- author.
Title: Texas / by John Hamilton.
Description: Minneapolis, MN : Abdo Publishing, [2017] | Series: The United
    States of America | Includes index.
Identifiers: LCCN 2015957741 | ISBN 978-1-68078-346-9 (lib. bdg.) |
    ISBN 9781680774504 (ebook)
Subjects: LCSH: Texas--Juvenile literature.
Classification: DDC 976.4--dc23
LC record available at http://lccn.loc.gov/2015957741

CONTENTS

THE
LONE STAR
STATE

Texas is so big, in both its land and economy, that it could be a country. In fact, Texas *was* a country during its early history. Today, it is a state with bustling cities and growing industries. Its vast landscape holds sprawling farms with cotton fields and grazing land for cattle. Texas's oil fields pump more black gold out of the Earth than any other state.

There's much more to Texas than just its land. Its people are a very diverse group. Yes, there are cowboys and rich oil barons, but there are also artists, musicians, athletes, scientists, and more, from all walks of life and many nationalities. Big-hearted Texans are fiercely independent, loyal, and always willing to lend a helping hand (especially when it comes to advice about BBQ sauce).

The Texas state flag includes a single white star. It represents the independent spirit of the state's people. That is why Texas is nicknamed "The Lone Star State."

Texas longhorns are a breed of cattle whose horns may extend up to 7 feet (2 m) from tip to tip.

Lost Mine Trail in
Big Bend National Park.

QUICK FACTS

Name: Texas is based on the Caddo Native American word *tejas*, which means "friends."

State Capital: Austin, population 931,830

Date of Statehood: December 29, 1845 (28th state)

Population: 27,469,114 (2nd-most populous state)

Area (Total Land and Water): 268,596 square miles (695,660 sq km), 2nd-largest state

Largest City: Houston, population 2,296,224

Nickname: The Lone Star State

Motto: Friendship

State Bird: Mockingbird

State Flower: Bluebonnet

State Stone: Petrified Palmwood

State Tree: Pecan

State Song: "Texas, Our Texas"

Highest Point: Guadalupe Peak, 8,749 feet (2,667 m)

Guadalupe Peak

Lowest Point: Gulf of Mexico, 0 feet (0 m)

Average July High Temperature: 94°F (34°C)

Gulf of Mexico

Record High Temperature: 120°F (49°C), in Monahans on June 28, 1994

Average January Low Temperature: 34°F (1°C)

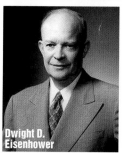
Dwight D. Eisenhower

Record Low Temperature: -23°F (-31°C), in Seminole on February 8, 1933

Average Annual Precipitation: 28 inches (71 cm)

Number of U.S. Senators: 2

Lyndon Johnson

Number of U.S. Representatives: 36

U.S. Presidents Born in Texas: Dwight D. Eisenhower (1890-1969); Lyndon B. Johnson (1908-1973)

U.S. Postal Service Abbreviation: TX

QUICK FACTS

GEOGRAPHY

Texas covers 268,596 square miles (695,660 sq km) of territory, second only to Alaska. It is in the south-central part of the United States. It has many kinds of natural environments, from the plains of the northern Panhandle, to pine forests, to the subtropical Lower Rio Grande Valley of the southeast.

Texas shares a border with New Mexico to the west. The Rio Grande forms a river border with Mexico to the south. To the north is the state of Oklahoma. The Red River makes up much of the Oklahoma border. To the east are Arkansas and Louisiana. The Sabine River forms most of the border with Louisiana. The large, crescent-shaped part of southeastern Texas borders the warm waters of the Gulf of Mexico.

The Rio Grande forms a river border between Texas and Mexico.

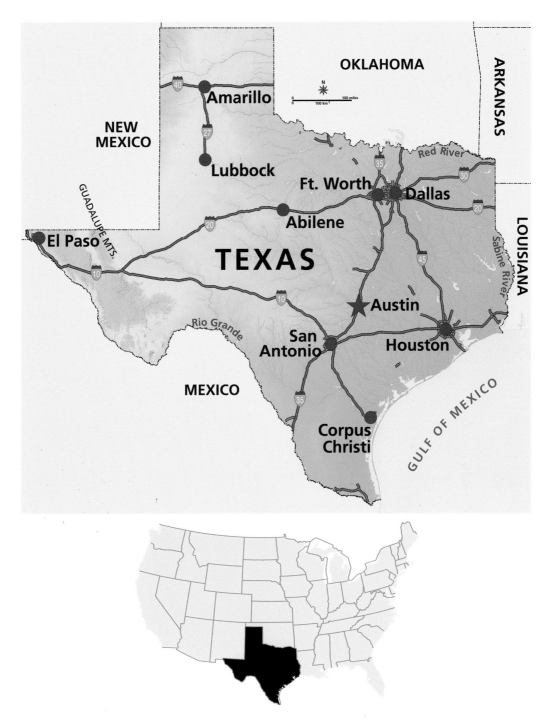

Texas's total land and water area is 268,596 square miles (695,660 sq km).

It is the 2nd-largest state. The state capital is Austin.

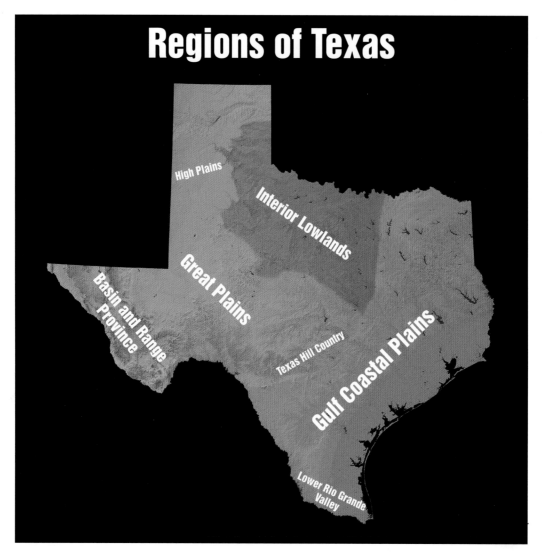

Regions of Texas

The Gulf Coastal Plains region is along the Gulf of Mexico in southeastern Texas. It covers almost 40 percent of the state, extending in some places more than 200 miles (322 km) inland from the Gulf of Mexico. The land is mostly flat, with pine forests and some rolling hills. Along the coast, there is moist soil that is good for farming. There are barrier islands and protected bays for port cities. The Lower Rio Grande Valley, in the extreme south, is warm and moist, which makes it an excellent place for growing citrus fruits and vegetables.

The Interior Lowlands region is in north-central Texas. There are rolling plains that are good for raising cattle, along with flat areas that make good farmland.

The Great Plains region includes the western two-thirds of the Texas Panhandle, plus a large section of the central part of the state. The High Plains of the Panhandle are in the north. This area is vast and flat. Around the cities of Amarillo and Lubbock are many farms that grow wheat, corn, sorghum, and cotton. Herds of cattle are also raised. Farther south is the Texas Hill Country. Steep, forested slopes made of limestone conceal many caverns under the Earth.

The Basin and Range Province is in the western part of Texas. The land is arid and rugged. The Guadalupe Mountains are in this region. They contain Guadalupe Peak, the highest point in Texas. It rises 8,749 feet (2,667 m) above sea level.

Guadalupe Mountains

CLIMATE AND
WEATHER

Because Texas is so big, and has so many kinds of landscapes, it also experiences all kinds of weather. In general, the Gulf Coastal Plains of the southeast have a subtropical climate. It is warm and humid. The west side of Texas, however, is drier and hotter. It resembles the desert climate of the American Southwest region.

Temperatures vary widely across the state. Statewide, the average July high temperature is 94°F (34°C). The highest

Heat waves often hit Texas in the summer.

temperature ever recorded in Texas was 120°F (49°C) in the town of Monahans on June 28, 1994. In winter, the average January low is 34°F (1°C). The record low occurred in the town of Seminole on February 8, 1933. On that day, the thermometer plunged to -23°F (-31°C).

A tornado moves across Highway 287 near Goodnight, Texas. More twisters whirl over Texas than any other state.

Statewide, Texas receives a yearly average of 28 inches (71 cm) of precipitation. The western regions receive much less rain and snow. In the far south, snow is extremely rare.

Thunderstorms are common in Texas. The north-central part of the state is in Tornado Alley. Twisters whirl over Texas an average of 155 times yearly, the most of any state. Destructive hurricanes can also blow in from the Gulf of Mexico.

CLIMATE AND WEATHER

PLANTS AND
ANIMALS

There is a huge variety of plant and animal life in Texas, thanks to the state's many ecosystems. There are dry deserts in the west, grasslands on the plains, dense woodlands in the east, and subtropical beaches on the Gulf of Mexico coast.

About 38 percent of the state's land area is covered by forests. That is roughly 60 million acres (24.3 million ha). That is a surprise to anyone who has only ever driven across the treeless high plains of the northern Panhandle. Most of Texas's densest forests are in the east, but trees are scattered throughout the state. In total, Texas has more forestland than any other state except Alaska.

There are many kinds of trees growing in Texas. They include oak, pine, hickory, sweet gum, cypress, walnut, elm, ash, cottonwood, magnolia, willow, and maple trees. Palms grow on the southern coast along the Gulf of Mexico. The official state tree is the pecan.

Garner State Park by the Frio River shows a wide variety of trees found in Texas.

Texas is well known for its grasslands. Native tallgrass prairies once covered much of the state. Today, most of the prairies have been converted to farmland. However, hundreds of species of grasses can still be found in Texas. They include buffalo grass, grama, switchgrass, Indiangrass, side oats, bluestem, and curly mesquite. Many kinds of cacti also grow in the state, especially in the arid Basin and Range Province of western Texas.

There are more than 5,000 kinds of flowering plants that bloom in Texas. The official state flower of Texas is the bluebonnet.

Texas is filled with flowering plants of all types.

Mexican free-tailed bats are Texas's state flying mammal. The bats roost together in caves, mines, wells, hollow trees, and even buildings and bridges.

Bison, black bears, mountain lions, elk, red wolves, and pronghorns are all native to Texas, and were once common. Unfortunately, overhunting and habitat reduction nearly caused them to disappear from the state. Hard-working conservation groups have ensured that some survive, either in pockets of remote wilderness or on protected wildlife preserves.

Mammals commonly found in Texas include bobcats, coyotes, white-tailed deer, mule deer, rabbits, skunks, wild pigs, raccoons, badgers, bats, foxes, gophers, opossums, squirrels, and armadillos.

American Alligator

More than 100 species of snakes can be found slithering across the ground in Texas. Venomous snakes include copperheads, rattlesnakes, cottonmouths, and Texas coral snakes. Other reptiles in Texas include horned lizards, Texas alligator lizards, and eastern collared lizards. American alligators are found in freshwater swamps and marshes along the Gulf of Mexico coast.

Common freshwater fish found swimming in Texas's lakes and rivers include largemouth and smallmouth bass, catfish, sunfish, crappies, bullheads, gar, and suckers.

About three-quarters of all bird species in the United States can be found in Texas. Common species include chickadees, screech owls, great horned owls, red-bellied woodpeckers, blue jays, cardinals, American robins, cormorants, egrets, herons, red-tailed hawks, crows, ravens, roadrunners, meadowlarks, and red-winged blackbirds.

Great Horned Owl

PLANTS AND ANIMALS

HISTORY

People came to the Texas area centuries before the first Europeans arrived in the early 1500s. The first people to live in the region probably arrived about 12,000 years ago, and perhaps much earlier. These nomadic Paleo-Indians were the ancient ancestors of today's Native Americans. They hunted animals, such as mammoths and giant bison, with stone spear points. As the centuries passed, they formed groups, or tribes, and lived in villages and learned to grow crops.

By the 1500s, several Native American tribes had established their homes in the Texas area. The Caddo tribe lived in eastern Texas. The Karankawa tribe lived along the Gulf of Mexico coast. The Apache tribe lived in western Texas. Other Native American tribes that eventually settled in Texas included the Comanche, Tonkawa, Cherokee, Shawnee, and others.

The Caddo tribe lived in eastern Texas, creating permanent villages beginning around 800 AD.

The Tejano Monument in Austin, Texas, shows symbols of the state's history, from Spanish explorer Alonso Álvarez de Pineda (far right), to a ranch owner on a mustang in the 1700s, to Tejano (Mexican-American) settlers with Texas longhorn cattle and other livestock.

In 1519, Spanish explorer and mapmaker Alonso Álvarez de Pineda was probably the first European to see present-day Texas. He was part of an expedition exploring the coast of the Gulf of Mexico. Other Spanish explorers soon entered the area, including Francisco Vásquez de Coronado. French explorers also ventured into eastern Texas from their settlements in neighboring Louisiana.

Starting in the late 1600s, Spanish settlers from Mexico came to Texas to build towns and Catholic missions. By 1718, the Spanish settlement of San Antonio was established. Other towns and missions included Nacogdoches, Goliad, and El Paso.

American settlers began moving into Texas in the early 1800s. At the time, Texas was controlled by Mexico's government, which welcomed settlers to the area.

In 1803, the United States bought a huge piece of land in the middle of the continent from France. It was called the Louisiana Purchase. (Today's state of Louisiana was just a small part of the area.) The sale almost doubled the land area of the United States. Part of today's Texas was included in the purchase, but the exact borders were disputed. Nevertheless, American settlers began moving into Texas.

In the early 1800s, Spain ruled Mexico. In 1821, Mexico won its freedom from Spain. Texas became a part of independent Mexico. The Mexican government allowed more American settlers into Texas. The settlers raised crops, and brought in tax money for Mexico.

In 1833, Antonio López de Santa Anna became the president of Mexico. He was unfriendly to American settlers in Texas. Fighting erupted between Mexican army troops and the Texans. Both the American settlers and many of the Mexicans who lived in Texas wanted freedom from Santa Anna's unjust laws.

Antonio López de Santa Anna was president of Mexico in the mid-1830s.

In 1836, the Texans revolted and declared their independence from Mexico. They called their new country the Republic of Texas. Mexican President Santa Anna sent thousands of soldiers to stop the rebellion. Today, it is called the Texas Revolution.

In February and March 1836, the Mexican army, led by Santa Anna himself, attacked a fort in San Antonio called the Alamo. The Texans held off the onslaught for nearly two weeks, but on March 6, 1836, all the Alamo's approximately 200 defenders were killed.

In 1836, Mexican forces attacked and overpowered defenders of the Alamo.

The Battle of the Alamo gave the Texans time to regroup and organize. Just a few weeks later, they defeated the Mexican army. Afterwards, the Republic of Texas named Sam Houston as president. Stephen Austin was named secretary of state.

Sam Houston, who led the Texas militia against Santa Anna's Mexican army, was elected the first president of the Republic of Texas in 1836.

The Republic of Texas lasted almost 10 years. The people decided it would be better to be part of the United States. The U.S. Congress agreed, and on December 29, 1845, Texas became the 28th state to join the Union.

When the Civil War (1861-1865) broke out, Texas lawmakers voted to secede, or leave, the Union. They decided to join 10 other Southern slave-owning states and form the Confederate States of America. Because Governor Sam Houston opposed secession, he was removed from office.

More than 70,000 Texans fought for the Confederacy. Few battles were fought in Texas itself. In 1865, the South lost the war, and the slaves were freed.

An oil gusher at Spindletop Hill, near Beaumont, Texas, around 1906.

After the Civil War, more people came to Texas. Farms sprang up, and railroad tracks were laid. Huge herds of cattle roamed the wide-open prairies. By 1900, more than three million people lived in the state.

In 1901, oil was discovered at Spindletop Hill, near the city of Beaumont. The state soon became a huge supplier of oil products. Even more people flocked to Texas.

During World War II (1939-1945), the Texas economy benefited. There was huge demand for oil and gas for the planes, ships, and other vehicles used to win the war.

In modern times, the economy of Texas has gone in many different directions. It remains the number-one producer of oil in the United States. Other industries are also big, including farming, tourism, manufacturing, and high-tech industries.

DID YOU KNOW?

• The Alamo was a Spanish mission that was turned into a fort near the present-day city of San Antonio, Texas. Between February 23 and March 6, 1836, it became the site of one of the most famous battles in American history. Months earlier, a group of armed Texans had occupied the fort as part of the Texas Revolution. Mexican President Santa Anna led nearly 2,000 of his soldiers to San Antonio and surrounded the Alamo. For 13 days, the brave men inside held off the Mexican army, even though they were far outnumbered. Finally, the onslaught was too much. Mexican soldiers climbed over the walls and overran the Texans. All the defenders were killed. Even soldiers who surrendered were executed. Among the dead were Colonel William Travis, Colonel James Bowie, and frontiersman Davy Crockett. A few weeks after the battle, Texas soldiers led by Sam Houston attacked Santa Anna's army at the Battle of San Jacinto on April 21, 1836. Their rallying cry was "Remember the Alamo!" The main battle lasted just 18 minutes. Santa Anna was captured. The victory ended Mexican rule over Texas.

• Texas is by far the leading cattle producer in the United States. The state had almost 12 million head of cattle in 2015. Some Texas ranches are huge. The King Ranch, near Corpus Christi, sprawls over 825,000 acres (333,866 ha), bigger than the land area of Rhode Island. The most famous breed of cattle is the Texas longhorn. These sturdy bovines can grow horns well over 7 feet (2.1 m) long from tip to tip.

• The Texas Rangers are the oldest statewide police force in the United States. Formed as a horse-mounted group of lawmen in 1835 to protect Texas's borderlands, the Rangers today investigate all kinds of crime, from murder to tracking down wanted fugitives. The fictional Lone Ranger was a former Texas Ranger.

DID YOU KNOW?

PEOPLE

Sam Houston (1793-1863) was a soldier and leader of early Texas. He was born in Virginia, but lived with Cherokee Native Americans in Tennessee when he was a teenager. The Cherokee nicknamed him "Black Raven." He gained military experience during the War of 1812 (1812-1815), when he met and became friends with future-president Andrew Jackson. Houston learned about politics from Jackson. Houston became a politician, served in Congress, and eventually was elected governor of Tennessee. In 1832, Houston moved to Texas. He arrived just as trouble began between the Mexican government and Texas settlers. He was chosen to lead Texas soldiers against Mexico in 1835. He defeated the Mexican army in 1836. He was elected president of the Republic of Texas, and later served as governor when the state was admitted to the Union. Today, the city of Houston, Texas, is named in his honor.

Stephen Austin (1793-1836) is known as the "Father of Texas" who was a leader in the settlement of the state. He was born in Virginia, raised in Missouri, and educated in Kentucky. He brought hundreds of American settlers to Texas by selling them cheap land. He worked as a diplomat between the Texans and the Mexican government. He tried to convince Mexico to give the Texas settlers more freedom to govern themselves. Instead, Austin was imprisoned for two years. After Texas won its independence from Mexico in 1836, Austin ran for president of the new Republic of Texas. He lost to Sam Houston, but served as secretary of state. Today, the Texas capital city of Austin is named in his honor.

Lyndon B. Johnson (1908-1973) was the 36th president of the United States. A Democrat, he served from 1963-1969. Before that, he was elected vice president in 1960, serving under President John F. Kennedy. In 1963, Johnson became president after Kennedy's assassination in Dallas, Texas. As president, Johnson helped pass civil rights and anti-poverty laws. He also championed education and conservation efforts. His final years in office were marred by America's involvement in the Vietnam War. Johnson was born in Stonewall, Texas.

Jim Parsons (1973-) is an actor best known for playing physicist Sheldon Cooper on the hit television comedy show *The Big Bang Theory*. He is also a talented stage and film actor. He was born in Houston, Texas. He started acting in school plays. After graduating, he acted in both New York City, New York, and Los Angeles, California. He first appeared as the quirky scientific genius Sheldon Cooper in 2007. Parsons has won four Emmy Awards for his work.

Kelly Clarkson (1982-) is a Grammy Award-winning singer and performer. Born in Fort Worth, Texas, she sang in the choir in high school. In 2002, she became the first winner on the talent search television show *American Idol.* The show catapulted her to pop superstardom. In 2004, her first album, *Breakaway,* had several hits, including "Since U Been Gone," "Breakaway," and "Walk Away." She has since recorded several more albums, and won many awards for her work, including three Grammy Awards.

Michael Strahan (1971-) was a defensive end for the NFL's New York Giants. He played for 15 seasons, from 1993 to 2007. Strahan was born in Houston, Texas. He played college ball at Texas Southern University in Houston. As a Giant, he was the NFL sack leader in 2001 and 2003. He holds the record for the most sacks in a season, with 22.5 sacks in 2001. After retirement, Strahan became a well-known football analyst and television talk and news show host.

CITIES

Austin is the capital of Texas. Its population is about 931,830. It is located in the east-central part of the state, along the Colorado River. First settled in 1835, its original name was Waterloo. It was renamed in 1839 in honor of Stephen Austin, the "Father of Texas." It officially became the state capital in 1846. Today, Austin is a fast-growing city. Dozens of high-tech businesses have operations in the Austin metropolitan area, including Dell, IBM, and Apple. There are several universities in the city, including the University of Texas at Austin, which enrolls more than 51,000 students annually. Austin has a very active music scene. There are many outdoor concerts and festivals held in the city, including South by Southwest, a unique festival of music, films, and interactive technologies.

Houston is the biggest city in Texas. Its population is about 2,296,224. With its suburbs and surrounding communities, the metropolitan area is home to approximately 6.5 million people. Houston is located in eastern Texas, very close to the Gulf of Mexico. A port city, Houston is connected to the Gulf of Mexico by deep bays and waterways. The city is named after Sam Houston, the first president of the Republic of Texas. Today, Houston is a leading center for transportation, manufacturing, aeronautics, and the oil and natural gas industries. The city is home to NASA's Lyndon B. Johnson Space Center, which includes the Mission Control Center for human space exploration. In downtown Houston, there are many art galleries, museums, orchestras, and theaters. The 55-acre (22-ha) Houston Zoo is home to more than 6,000 animals.

Dallas is the third-largest city in Texas. Located in the north-central part of the state, its population is approximately

1,300,092. Together with its suburbs and surrounding communities, including the cities of Fort Worth and Arlington, the metropolitan area is home to more than 7.1 million people. Dallas is known for banking, manufacturing, electronic equipment, oil, and medical products. The city is famous for Tex-Mex cuisine and barbecue sauce. Downtown Dallas has many galleries and performing arts centers.

San Antonio is the second-most populated city in Texas. It is home to about 1,469,845 people. It is located in south-central Texas. The city's economy depends on energy, health care, banking, manufacturing, and tourism. The Alamo is one of the most-visited sites in the state. The River Walk is a wide, paved walkway along the San Antonio River. There are many pleasant cafes and shops along the walkway, which was built below street level to cut down on road noise.

El Paso is the sixth-largest city in Texas. Its population is about 681,124. It is located in far-western Texas, along the Rio Grande. Across the river is the city of Juarez, Mexico. Top employers include government, education, health care, data processing, and manufacturing. The Fiesta de las Flores, the area's oldest Hispanic festival, features regional food and art. At the U.S. Army's Fort Bliss, tank crews learn to fight and maneuver in desert terrain.

Corpus Christi is the eighth-largest city in Texas, with a population of about 324,074. Is is located in the southeastern part of the state, along the Gulf Coast. Tourism and oil are the city's biggest industries. A large, deepwater port handles massive amounts of petrochemicals and agricultural goods. North Beach is home to the Texas State Aquarium and the retired USS *Lexington* aircraft carrier, which is a museum ship today.

TRANSPORTATION

There are 313,228 miles (504,092 km) of public roadways in Texas. That is more than any other state. Several interstate highways crisscross Texas. Interstate I-35 begins in Laredo, on the Mexican border. It travels all the way north to Duluth, Minnesota. Interstate I-10 runs east and west in southern Texas, passing through the cities of Houston, San Antonio, and El Paso. Interstate I-20 runs east and west through central Texas, passing through Dallas, Fort Worth, and Abilene. Running east and west across the northern Panhandle is Interstate I-40, which passes through Amarillo.

There are 49 freight railroads operating in Texas on 10,469 miles (16,848 km) of track. The most common goods hauled by rail include chemicals, coal, stone, oil, and farm products.

A freight train runs parallel to a highway near Shallowater, Texas.

Container ships are unloaded at the busy Port of Houston.

Dozens of seaports along Texas's long Gulf of Mexico coastline serve cargo and passenger vessels, as well as fishing fleets. The leading deepwater ports for cargo ships are in Houston, Beaumont, Corpus Christi, and Texas City. The Gulf Intracoastal Waterway is an inland shipping lane protected from ocean waves. Barge traffic uses the waterway along the coast from Brownsville, Texas, all the way to Florida.

There are hundreds of airports in Texas. Dallas-Fort Worth International Airport is one of the busiest airports in the nation. It handles approximately 64 million passengers each year.

Dallas-Fort Worth International Airport

NATURAL
RESOURCES

Texas is the nation's number-one producer of oil and natural gas. The state's 27 refineries have a processing capacity of 5.1 million barrels of crude oil daily. That is almost a third of the entire country's refining ability. The state is also a leader in wind energy production, and in coal mining. Other minerals mined in Texas include sulfur, lead, zinc, magnesium, sulfur, gypsum, plus sand and gravel.

Texas is an agricultural powerhouse. There are about 242,000 farms in the state, the most in the nation. The average farm size is 537 acres (217 ha). In total, Texas farms and ranches cover about 130 million acres (52.6 million ha) of land, about 76 percent of the state.

An oil refinery outside of Houston, Texas.

Ranch hands drive cattle in Andrews County, Texas. The state is the number-one producer of cattle.

Texas is the country's number-one producer of cotton and cattle. Other top agricultural products include corn for livestock, hay, sorghum, wheat, peanuts, rice, broiler chickens, turkeys, nursery plants, plus a variety of fruits and vegetables. Texas is also the number-one producer of Angora goats. Their hair is used to make a silky fabric called mohair.

Angora Goat

Most of Texas's forest industry is located in the eastern part of the state. Lumber and paper mills in the area employ thousands of Texans.

Commercial fishing takes place in the Gulf of Mexico. A wide variety of seafood is caught, including shrimp, oysters, snapper, crabs, and Atlantic croaker.

NATURAL RESOURCES

INDUSTRY

Raising cattle, producing oil, and growing cotton are all big industries in Texas. However, the largest part of the state's economy is the service industry. Instead of making products, companies in the service industry sell services to other businesses and consumers. It includes businesses such as banking, financial services, health care, insurance, restaurants, and tourism. About 58 percent of working Texans are employed in the service industry.

Texas manufacturers produce many kinds of goods. The state is a leading maker of computers, as well as telecommunications and other electronic equipment. Health care is also a big industry. The Texas Medical Center, in Houston, is one of the biggest medical research and care centers in the world.

In 1925, Memorial Hermann was the first hospital to open in what is today the vast Texas Medical Center. This Houston-based medical research and care center sees more than 160,000 people each day.

At Johnson Space Center Mission Control, flight controllers support NASA activities such as International Space Station missions and spacecraft launches.

Vacationers are attracted to Texas's many fun and historic sites, including the Alamo, Big Bend National Park, San Antonio's River Walk, and the beaches along South Padre Island. More than 255 million people visit the Lone Star State each year. Visitors spend about $69 billion annually and support 653,000 jobs.

The National Aeronautics and Space Administration (NASA) has a large facility near Houston called the Lyndon B. Johnson Space Center. American astronauts are trained at the center, which has more than 100 buildings and employs thousands of workers. It is also home to Mission Control Center, the flight control facility made famous during the Apollo Moon missions.

SPORTS

The Dallas Cowboys and the Houston Texans play in the National Football League (NFL). The Cowboys are nicknamed "America's Team." They have won the Super Bowl five times.

The Dallas Mavericks, the San Antonio Spurs, and the Houston Rockets shoot hoops in the National Basketball Association (NBA). The Spurs have won five NBA Finals championships. The Rockets have won twice, and the Mavericks have won once. The San Antonio Stars play in the Women's National Basketball Association (WNBA).

The Texas Rangers and the Houston Astros are Major League Baseball (MLB) teams. The Dallas Stars skate in the National Hockey League (NHL). They won the Stanley Cup championship during the 1998-99 season. Other professional sports in Texas include soccer, automobile racing, golfing, rodeo, plus many others.

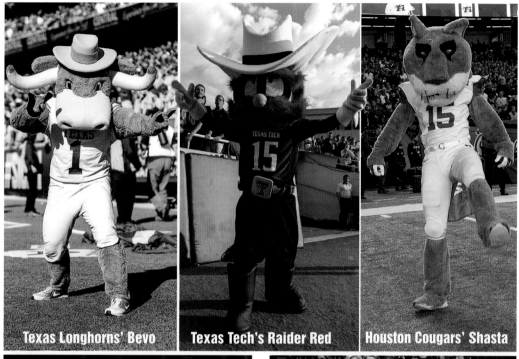

Texas Longhorns' Bevo Texas Tech's Raider Red Houston Cougars' Shasta

Texas Aggies' Reveille

Baylor Bears' Bruiser

High school and college sports are big in Texas, especially football. There are dozens of popular college teams. They include the Texas Longhorns from the University of Texas at Austin, the Texas Aggies from Texas A&M University in College Station, the Red Raiders from Texas Tech University in Lubbock, the Houston Cougars from the University of Houston, and the Baylor Bears from Baylor University in Waco, Texas.

Outdoor sports are hugely popular in Texas. For hikers and campers, there are two national parks, both in the western part of the state. They are Big Bend National Park and Guadalupe Mountains National Park.

ENTERTAINMENT

Most of Texas's large cities have art museums, orchestras, and live theaters. Because its people come from so many cultures, the state's museums and art centers reflect much diversity.

The State Fair of Texas has been held at Fair Park in Dallas since 1886. For three weeks each autumn, more than 2.6 million people come for the thrill rides, finger-licking-good BBQ and deep-fried delicacies, and to catch a glimpse of Big Tex, the 55-foot (17-m) tall mascot of the State Fair since 1952.

Big Tex

Six Flags OVER TEXAS

Six Flags Over Texas features such thrill rides as the Texas Giant, the tallest steel hybrid roller coaster in the world.

The Dallas World Aquarium features huge tanks with walk-through tunnels where visitors can see marine life from all over the world. There is also a rainforest exhibit with many kinds of birds, such as toucans and ibises, plus fish, mammals, and tropical plant life.

Six Flags Over Texas, in Arlington, has shows, shopping, and dozens of thrill rides, including 12 roller coasters. SeaWorld San Antonio is an aquatic theme park. There are many rides, exhibits, and shows to learn about killer whales, sea lions, dolphins, and other sea creatures.

Fiesta San Antonio was first held in 1891. Today, more than 3.5 million people come to celebrate San Antonio's diverse culture. There are dozens of events all over the city, including colorful parades, concerts, sporting contests, and walking tours of the Alamo.

TIMELINE

10,000 BC—The first nomadic Paleo-Indians arrive in the present-day area of Texas.

1500s—Caddo, Karankawa, and Apache Native Americans settle in the Texas area.

1519—Spanish explorer Alonso Álvarez de Pineda is probably the first European to see the coast of present-day Texas.

1718—Spanish settlement of San Antonio, Texas, established.

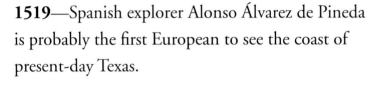

1803—The United States buys a large portion of land from France, which includes a part of Texas. It is called the Louisiana Purchase.

1821—Newly independent Mexico allows American settlers to move into Texas.

1836—Texans declare independence from Mexico. Mexican forces overpower Texans in the Battle of the Alamo. Other Texans fight the Mexican army. The Republic of Texas wins its independence.

1845—Texas becomes the 28th state to join the Union.

1900—The Galveston Hurricane makes landfall near the city of Galveston, Texas, killing approximately 8,000 people. It is the country's deadliest natural disaster.

1901—Oil is discovered at Spindletop Hill. The huge deposit marks the beginning of Texas's rise as a major oil producer.

1963—NASA officially opens the Manned Spacecraft Center in Houston. It is renamed Lyndon B. Johnson Space Center in 1973, after the former U.S. president.

1996—The Dallas Cowboys win their fifth Super Bowl championship (for the 1995 season).

2000—Former Texas Governor George W. Bush is elected president of the United States, serving from 2001-2009.

2014—The San Antonio Spurs win their fifth NBA Finals championship (for the 2013-14 season).

2015—Five years of drought come to an end as torrential rains drench Texas. Flooding destroys hundreds of homes and kills at least 21 people.

GLOSSARY

Alamo

A fort and former Spanish mission in San Antonio where a battle for Texas independence was fought in 1836.

Barrier Islands

Long, narrow landforms just offshore from a mainland. Barrier islands are usually made up of sand, silt, and pebbles.

Battle of San Jacinto

An important battle of the Texas Revolution, which was fought on April 21, 1836. The Texas defenders defeated Mexican forces, giving Texas independence.

Ecosystem

A biological community of animals, plants, and bacteria who live together in the same physical or chemical environment.

Gulf Coast

The area of southeastern Texas that borders the Gulf of Mexico.

Gulf Intracoastal Waterway

A shipping lane that goes along the Gulf Coast, from Brownsville, Texas, to Florida.

Louisiana Purchase

A purchase by the United States from France in 1803 of a huge section of land west of the Mississippi River. The United States nearly doubled in size after the purchase. The young country paid $15 million for approximately 828,000 square miles (2.1 million sq km) of land.

MISSION

A large building or fort that Christians used as a base to spread their religion to the local people. Spanish missions in Texas were also used to help govern the new colony.

NATIONAL AERONAUTICS AND SPACE ADMINISTRATION (NASA)

A U.S. government agency started in 1958. NASA's goals include space exploration, as well as increasing people's understanding of Earth, our solar system, and the universe.

PANHANDLE

The northern part of Texas. It is an area of land that juts out from the rest of the state. The city of Amarillo is in the center of the Texas Panhandle.

PLAINS

A large, flat area of land. There are few trees, but plains often have grasslands.

REPUBLIC OF TEXAS

An independent country that withdrew from the control of Mexico in 1836, and lasted until it became a state of the United States in 1845.

TEX-MEX

A kind of cooking that blends flavors of regional food from Texas and Mexico.

TORNADO ALLEY

An area of the United States that has many tornadoes. There is no official boundary for Tornado Alley. Many maps show that it stretches from Texas in the south to North Dakota in the north. Some say it reaches to Ohio.

WORLD WAR II

A conflict that was fought from 1939 to 1945, involving countries around the world. The United States entered the war after Japan bombed the American naval base at Pearl Harbor, in Oahu, Hawaii, on December 7, 1941.

INDEX